COMMENTS ON THE POEMS OF GERALD COSTANZO

"*Nobody Lives on Arthur Godfrey Boulevard* is highly idiosyncratic, a wry and quirky sequence of poems that portrays America as the fever dream of a media network stoned out of its mind. Costanzo offers parables, fables, jokes, and put-ons—and yet his book is serious in intention and memorable in expression. It is great fun to read."

    —Fred Chappell, *The Georgia Review*

"Gerald Costanzo is the literary son of Nathanael and Mae West."

    —Richard Katrovas

"This is truly poetry in the American grain. Costanzo looks unflinchingly at our totems, artifacts, and folkways and sets them down just as they are, with a deadly but affectionate irony."

    —Carolyn Kizer

"[These poems] make clear that the source of Costanzo's empathy for the culture lies in the fact that he refuses to separate himself from the waywardness and shortcomings he sees in the world around him. . . . Costanzo mourns a culture where genuine emotion cannot be found, but where its semblance can be endlessly marketed. [His] final vision is of a human story whose meaning and redemption lie in the struggle one goes on making—out of flawed intentions and broken gestures, exile and uncertain return, out of provisional, partial knowledge—to imagine something whole, complete."

    —Deborah Pope, *The Southern Review*

"There is an odd nostalgia in Costanzo's poems . . . and ironic insinuations in the last lines."

    —*Publisher's Weekly*

"These poems are wonderful. Smart, funny, irreverent, lyrical—and a great pleasure to read."

    —Charles Simic

T0326759

"Gerald Costanzo writes about the real America, not white picket fences lurking with roses outside Des Moines, but a better and truer place where our bulky prehistoric myths echo through the smog like the names of the famously dead, where the blind count our money, where the halt and the lame are healed by the insane. I love these poems. Even better, I believe them."

—James Crumley

"Gerald Costanzo takes a cool attitude toward his subject matter: he is at once the man lecturing at the podium and the delinquent dozing off at the back of the hall."

—Ron Slate, *The Chowder Review*

"Gerald Costanzo demonstrates what many of us have long known, that of all our poets he is by far the best satirist. . . . [His] verbal tactics are not safe, because he lets his rage and indignation peep out a little. Such emotions are present in the pure extravagance of his imagination, an imagination perhaps as powerful as that of the late Philip K. Dick."

—Jonathan Holden in *On Moral Poetry*

"Costanzo is a grief-ridden observer of the *kulchur*. He reminds us of what we had, what we lost, perhaps what we never knew—and he does it in a mature, wise, lovely cadence. He is smart yet humble, full of pity for all of us, full of amazement. 'When I first heard about America,' he says, 'it was already too late.' He is one of our prophets."

—Gerald Stern

"Costanzo's wit and satire and vision of the grotesque world of America get to the center of much of the madness of our culture."

—Peter Balakian

REGULAR HAUNTS

TED KOOSER CONTEMPORARY POETRY | *Editor:* Ted Kooser

Regular Haunts

New and Previous Poems

GERALD COSTANZO

Introduction by Ted Kooser

UNIVERSITY OF NEBRASKA PRESS | LINCOLN AND LONDON

Acknowledgments for the use of copyrighted
material appear on pages xi–xiv, which
constitute an extension of the copyright page.

Publication of this volume was made possible
in part by the generous support of the
H. Lee and Carol Gendler Charitable Fund.

Library of Congress Cataloging-in-Publication Data
Names: Costanzo, Gerald, author.
Kooser, Ted, writer of introduction.
Title: Regular haunts: new and previous poems /
Gerald Costanzo; introduction by Ted Kooser.
Description: Lincoln: University of Nebraska Press,
2018. | Series: Ted Kooser contemporary poetry
Identifiers: LCCN 2017044549
ISBN 9781496205865 (pbk.: alk. paper)
ISBN 9781496206558 (epub)
ISBN 9781496206565 (mobi)
ISBN 9781496206572 (pdf)
Classification: LCC PS3553.O762 A6 2018
DDC 811/.54—dc23 LC record available
at https://lccn.loc.gov/2017044549

Set in Whitman by Mikala R Kolander.
Designed by N. Putens.

For my children,
Lizabeth and Michael-James,
and for my grandsons,
Mac and Cash

CONTENTS

PREVIOUS POEMS

I. THE SACRED COWS OF LOS ANGELES

ACKNOWLEDGMENTS

Grateful acknowledgment is made to editors of the following periodicals and anthologies in which the new poems first appeared. *Cold-Drill* (Boise State University): "The Longest Second" and "The Winter People"; *Great River Review*: "Deathgrass at the Wheeler Summerfest," "Tinnitus," "The Lives They Lead," "Stories," and "Havana Run"; *Gulf Steam Magazine*: "Deadline at Dawn" and "Blood of Poets"; *Heatherstone Poets Anniversary Anthology*: "The Big Heat," "Stairway to an Empty Room," and "A Graveyard to Let"; *The Hopkins Review*: "Minnie's Death" and "Hinky Dinky Parlay Voo"; *North Atlantic Review*: "Invitation to Violence," "The Out Is Death," and "Judge Me Not"; *North Dakota Quarterly*: "Provincetown" and "American River"; *Pittsburgh Tribune Review*: "Spend Game"; *Ploughshares*: "Arabesques and Bottle Blondes," "Memory and Loss," and "Blood on the Moon"; *The Portland Review*: "The Gentle Hangman" and "Downtown"; *Volt*: "City of Whispering Stone" and "Spend Game."

Poems in the "Regular Haunts" section were written with regard to my interest in rhyme and as a result of my passion for reading mystery novels and thrillers. Poem titles come from the title of the particular novel, and its author is attributed in parentheses. My method has been to appropriate the first sentences and break them into stanzas, thereby arriving at the rhymes. Sometimes the poems' themes are taken from the novels and sometimes from some world of their own. The novels from which the first sentences are taken were first published as follows: *The Big Heat* by William P. McGivern (New York: Dodd, Mead, 1952); *Blood on the Moon* by James

Ellroy (New York: The Mysterious Press, 1984); *Stairway to an Empty Room* by Dolores Hitchens (Garden City NY: Doubleday, 1951); *A Graveyard to Let* by Carter Dickson [John Dickson Carr] (New York: William Morrow, 1949); *Downtown* by Ed McBain (Evan Hunter) (New York: William Morrow, 1991); *The Longest Second* by Bill S. Ballinger (New York: Harper & Row, 1957); *The Out Is Death* by Peter Rabe (New York: Fawcett, 1957); *Blood of Poets* by Kenn Davis (New York: Fawcett, 1990); *City of Whispering Stone* by George Chesbro (New York: Simon & Schuster, 1978); *Judge Me Not* by John D. MacDonald (Greenwich CT: Gold Medal, 1951); *The Gentle Hangman* by James M. Fox (Boston: Little, Brown, 1950); *The Winter People* by Phyllis A. Whitney (New York: Doubleday, 1969); *Invitation to Violence* by Lionel White (New York: Dutton, 1958); *Deadline at Dawn* by William Irish [Cornell Woolrich] (Philadelphia: J. P. Lippincott, 1944); *Havana Run* by Les Standiford (New York: Putnam, 2003); and *Spend Game* by Jonathan Gash [John Grant] (New Haven CT: Ticknor & Fields, 1981).

The previous poems were first published in *Beloit Poetry Journal, Carolina Quarterly, Chowder Review, Colorado Review, Epoch, The Georgia Review, Gulfstream, Happiness Holding Tank, Intro 3* (edited by R. V. Cassill, New York: Bantam and McCall, 1970), *Kansas Quarterly, Kayak, Memphis State Review, The Midwest Quarterly, Minnesota Review, Mississippi Review, The Missouri Review, Mundus Artium, The Nation, New Salt Creek Reader, North American Review, North Dakota Quarterly, Oconee Review, Ohio Review, Ploughshares, Poetry Now, Poetry Texas, Prairie Schooner, The Sole Proprietor, Southern California Review, Spectrum, TransPacific, West Coast Poetry Review,* and *Willow Springs.* My enduring gratitude to the editors of these magazines and anthologies.

"The Sacred Cows of Los Angeles," "Snake," "Introduction to the Shopping Cart," "Houdini Disappearing in Philadelphia," "Newlywed," "The Resurrection of Lake Erie," "Dinosaurs of the Hollywood Delta," "The Riot of Nickel Beer Night," "Nobody Lives on Arthur Godfrey Boulevard," "The Rise of the Sunday School Movement," "Braille," "Seeing My Name in *TV*

"What's Wrong with the Moon" was first published in *My Poor Elephant*, edited by Eve Shelnutt, (Atlanta: Longstreet Press, 1992); "Braille" appeared in the *Anthology of Magazine Verse and Yearbook of American Poetry*, edited by Alan F. Pater (Los Angeles: Monitor Books, 1981); "Dinosaurs of the Hollywood Delta" appeared in *The Pushcart Prize X: Best of the Small Presses*, edited by Bill Henderson (New York: Pushcart Press/Viking-Penguin, 1985) and in the *Anthology of Magazine Verse and Yearbook of American Poetry*, edited by Alan F. Pater (Los Angeles: Monitor Books, 1985); "The Rise of the Sunday School Movement" appeared in *The Pushcart Prize XII: Best of the Small Presses*, edited by Bill Henderson (New York: Pushcart Press/ Viking-Penguin, 1987); "Nobody Lives on Arthur Godfrey Boulevard" and "Introduction of the Shopping Cart" appeared in *The Morrow Anthology of Younger American Poets*, edited by Dave Smith and David Bottoms (New York: William Morrow, 1985); "Seeing My Name in *TV Guide*" and "In the Blood" appeared in *Sometime the Cow Kick Your Head: Light Year '88/9*, edited by Robert Wallace (Cleveland: Bits Press, 1989); "The Sacred Cows of Los Angeles" appeared in *Gridlock: An Anthology of Poetry About Southern California*, edited by Elliott Fried (Los Angeles: Applezaba Press, 1990); "The Man Who Invented Las Vegas" appeared in *Traveling America with Today's Poets*, edited by David Kherdian (New York: Macmillan, 1977); "Dinosaurs of the Hollywood Delta" and "Excavating the Ruins of Miami Beach" appeared in *Decade Dance: A Celebration of Poems*, edited by Mark Sanders (Ord NE: Sandhills Press, 1991); "The Meeting" appeared in *Experiencing Poetry* by Eileen Thompson (New York: The Globe Book Company, 1987); "Dinosaurs of the Hollywood Delta" appeared in *From Here We Speak: An Anthology of Oregon Poetry*, edited by Ingrid Wendt and Primus St. John (Corvallis: Oregon State University Press, 1993); "Everything You Own" appeared in *The Gift of Tongues: Twenty-Five Years of Poetry from Copper Canyon Press*, edited by Sam Hamill (Port Townsend WA: Copper Canyon Press, 1996); "Near Lacombe" and "The Man Who Invented Las Vegas" appeared in *Oakland Review Anthology*, edited by Stacey W. Jenkins, Chris Holly, and Michael Plocek (Pittsburgh: *Oakland Review*, 1998); "Near Lacombe," "For Four Newsmen Murdered in Saigon," "In the Aviary," "My Kindergarten Girlfriend," "At Irony's Picnic," "The Bigamist," "When Guy Lombardo Died," and "The Meeting" appeared in *The Devins Award Poetry Anthology*, edited by Gerald Costanzo (Columbia: University of Missouri Press, 1998); "The Old Neighborhood" appeared in *Outsiders: Poems About Rebels, Exiles, and Renegades*, edited by Laure-Anne Bosselaar (Minneapolis: Milkweed Editions, 1999); "Washington Park" appeared in *Urban Nature: Poems about Wildlife in the City*, edited by Laure-Anne Bosselaar (Minneapolis: Milkweed Editions, 2000); "Bournehurst-on-the-Canal," "The Story," and "Excavating the Ruins of Miami Beach" appeared in *It's Not You, It's Me: The Poetry of Breakup*, edited by Jerry Williams (New York: The Overlook Press, 2010). The author acknowledges the Carmen Balcells Literary Agency, Barcelona, Spain, for permission to quote three lines from "World's End" by Pablo Neruda as an epigraph for the poem "Deathgrass at the Wheeler Summerfest."

I would like to express my gratitude to the National Endowment for the Arts for two Creative Writing Fellowships during which time many of these poems were written. I am indebted as well to the Pennsylvania Council on the Arts for an Individual Fellowship award.

A few of the "previous" poems, when first published in magazines, carried the following dedications that I wish to acknowledge here: "The Old Neighborhood" is for Gerald Stern; "Snake" for Susan Petrie; "The Resurrection of Lake Erie" for William Boggs; "Landscape with Unemployed Jockeys" for Allyson Hunter; "Washington Park" for Grace McGinnis; " Manhattan as a Latin America Capital" for Sally Cortese and Annamae Lawson; "Report from the Past" for Ted Hammett; and "Toward San Francisco" for Carla.

Thanks to Mark Luczak, Cynthia Lamb, and Connie Amoroso for help in preparing this book.

INTRODUCTION
Ted Kooser

Wit in contemporary American poetry comes in a couple of flavors. There's jokey writing, smart and fresh and original, fun to read and to hear the poet read, in which the central purpose is not only to entertain but also to show off the author's cleverness. With jokey writing you feel the poet out in front of the poem, saying, "Hey, it's all about me! See how clever I am!" Read a poem like that just once and that's enough. You get it; you got it.

The second type is also smart and fresh and original and fun to read, and fun to hear the poet read, but it's not about the poet or about the poet's cleverness. The poet stands well out of the way. These poems suggest some other presence, some moving shadow drifting along a little way under the surface. You can't quite see it clearly, but you sense it's there.

What that something is, of course, is poetry. For poetry, a meaningful experience that happens within a reader as he or she reads a poem is not always available from every poem a reader comes upon. A verse can be only a verse, something that can ring sweetly, like a bell, but once the ringing is gone the bell goes hollow.

Real poetry is only rarely found on the surface, in the dazzle of wit. Instead, it runs along under the laughter, beneath the delight, making us feel slightly uneasy, vaguely unsettled, as if we were being very artfully eased into a deeper and even a dangerous place. Many of the poems you'll find in this book are excellent examples of this. You can feel a hand on your elbow, gently urging you forward, nudging you maybe a little too close to the railing on the lee side of the deck.

I've been following Jerry Costanzo's writing for forty years and have never felt satisfied reading his poems just once. There's that delightful surface, sparkling with wit, with satire, with wordplay, and then there's always that something else, that mystery maybe a fathom beneath the sun on the waves.

The book you're holding is both a delight and a sounding: a delight to read for pleasure, and a sounding, as in when you let out a rope with a weight on the end and let it bounce along over the bottom, stirring up something. Here wit's in service to an end beyond wit.

One of many good examples of this is "Provincetown," which I love for its ability to picture a famous, exclusive arts and tourist community with a few deftly selected words. If you look at this poem closely, it's not only about the Provincetown a person can see from a street corner but what's deep beneath it, behind it, around it. Oh, yes, the psychiatrists have arrived in full fashion but, oh, why is it they've come? We have a poet here with X-ray vision.

I'm extremely pleased to have had the opportunity to follow these poems through to publication. Like the other books in this series, *Regular Haunts* is a selection from many years of writing and publishing, poems that have already tested the water and found it safe to walk upon. With the three earlier books, we now have a very good start at a University of Nebraska Press representation of the wide and exciting range of contemporary American poetry.

REGULAR HAUNTS

NEW POEMS

I.

American River

Arabesques and Bottle Blondes

The Scheherazades played bridge every
Thursday afternoon. Probably there were
reasons for this as the ladies in the group
might, on occasion, attest. The sea was there
before them, its meaning immeasurable.
After a twelfth trick, the one most beautiful
surprised by confessing there had been
no "relations" for six years. Some nervous
laughter, of course, and the one who was once
Miss Duluth was positive it wasn't true
and could not resist saying so.
Still, the waves sparkled and beckoned;
the mojitos, served beside the potted bougainvillea,
had been a fine idea. And truly there is always
more than meets the eye when trump
is to be determined. Their evenings were cool
and those sunsets obvious as an ace of hearts.
This was the dream of gaming in sublime climate,
and Florida, they knew, is mostly weather.

Provincetown

August. The psychiatrists
are arriving. Steerage of Cadillac-
and Mercedes-with-New-York-plates
along Commercial Street. The little
yard edged with white picket
at the foot of Gosnold
aflutter with pigeons and assiduous
afternoon light. Then the Löwenbräu
truck, loaded with the Special
and the Dark, backs—painstakingly
is the only way to say it—into the narrow
alley next to Vorelli's. The driver,
hooted down by halted youth
dressed in Bart Simpsonware,
makes it via the usual hairs-
breadth method and suddenly
life is good again.

Welcome back. Welcome back, doctors!

American River

We were talking about the man
who stole California from the Mexicans
and his carpenter who discovered
gold in the sawmill trailrace
at the little presidio
on the American.

Then it was all squatters and harlots,
and the way the rush for gold
becomes a rush for everything else:
Hollywood Freeway, Santa Ana
Wind, Tarzana, the first homicide
in Tomorrowland.

American multitude
staking its claim. Easy come.
Farmers, muggers, mechanics, and thieves
converging at the banks,
entirely guiltless of any knowledge
of mining.

Mrs. Alexander Graham Bell

In memory of James Tate

If we're pushing for the countenance
of a woman to adorn the currency of these
United States, I'd favor the venerable Eleanor
Roosevelt on the twenty, or maybe
Hillary Rodham Clinton on the five
thousand dollar bill so we won't have to see
her so often. Perhaps a national referendum
on which bank lady might embody the most Trust
in God. Edna St. Vincent Millay would
still be beautiful on the fifty, and Rosa Parks—
or how about my grandmother, Mrs.
Alexander Graham Bell, on
the sawbuck? That way each time we'd pull
one of her out of our billfolds, there
she'd be, bearing the same expression
she always assumed just after
exclaiming, *I thought I told you never
to say that!* or *Please finish
your soup before leaving
the table.*

Deathgrass at the Wheeler Summerfest

> I chose an ambiguous country
> where no one had heard
> of tomatoes or Norwegians.
> —Pablo Neruda

Robert was an administrator
till he got the pink slip that said
"see ya later." I'm sure glad I caught
your eye while you were stopped for that light.
It wasn't gremlins you were seein' last night,
it was Gertie's Hummel collection—I'm just sayin'.
It wasn't the Beatles who were prophetic;
it was the Beau Brummels. Some days it's
all alibis and crocodile tears. And "prostitute" is an absolute
rhyme with "cute." Or it takes the train all day
just to get past the grocery store. Things are getting
better now that things are getting worse; our boys
still being sent overseas. They come back
to rest in peace. No one writes good songs
about the war.

Tinnitus

Bearers of this malady are advised by current medical
thinking to embrace the condition and move on.
        —Wikipedia

I used to think the world
was round, but the Somali pirates
have proven it doesn't matter.
Nor does that outbreak of tinnitus—
the national epidemic—
people everywhere hearing more
of the implausible. Too
bad they believe it.
The schoolmaster who looked
like Art Garfunkel
was telling the children
There will be no more of that!
And there wasn't. Now give
us a kiss. Don't smile, for gosh
sake, just say *cheese*.

Memory and Loss

For Miroslav Nikolov

In the year I graduated
from West Daffodil Sr. High School
there was so much romance
in the hallways
that, by the end, the powers
that be, weary of it all,
cancelled the prom. This forced
us to explore each other's
undraped bodies exclusively
in such automobiles
and private homes as the district
afforded. The moral here
is not what you think. It isn't really
about memory and loss. Maybe
it's about the events of our lives
that remain hidden even from
ourselves. I was a Tiger. I was a
starting senior. Before it all
came down I had driven to Leesburg
to buy a tuxedo.

Hinky Dinky Parlay Voo

I finally figured out why
Kitty Dukakis drank rubbing alcohol—
life's ponderables being imponderable
as they mostly are. Why in competitive cheering
a cheerleader's worst nightmare
is an illegal tower. Why,
in that beautiful language of theirs,
the deaf love the sign
for New Orleans.

The Lives They Lead

For Cynthia

It was one of those late-summer evenings
far from the city. They took their supper
at the lodge; drove to the little theater

in the woods.
Soon after the play began—
thunder, and rain on the metal roof

came down so hard no one could hear
the actors' words. When the din
lingered and the mime,

they began to imagine the story—
as one would. They were able.
They made do. They nearly understood.

Stories

How I loved it when,
Those evenings together before bed,
I'd open a book to begin—
And my little girl and my little
Boy, no matter what it had been,
Would, shoulder to shoulder, call out
Read it again!

Minnie's Death

Mickey is sitting on a stool in the Crow's Nest, a bar in L.A.
He's drinking a beer. He needs something stronger. He is
suicidal. He never married her and now she's dead. He can't
believe it. He's reading her obituary in the *Times*: Minerva
Mouse (1928–2016), in Hollywood. Daughter of the late
Marcus Mouse and a late, unnamed mother. Loving aunt of
twin nieces Millie Mouse and Melody Mouse. She is survived
by her longtime significant other, Mickey Mouse, and her black-
and-white kitten, Figaro, whom she found abandoned on
Doheny Avenue. Mickey is beside himself. He asks the barkeep
for a yellow, No. 2 pencil. He is contemplating erasing
his wrists.

II.

Regular Haunts

*Brief poems ending with the first sentences
of mystery novels and thrillers*

(There was a transition in taste in popular literature in America during the
1940s—from Westerns to mystery novels. In the midst of this transition came
numerous amalgams such as *Sleuths in Spurs* and *The West Texas Mystery*.)

It was known that Fargo upon these occasions betook himself to
a hideout with a couple of books of poetry and a large quantity of
liquor, and read poetry and drank whiskey until he was stupefied with
both. When he recovered he would return to his regular haunts.
—Frank Gruber, *The Silver Tombstone Mystery* (1945)

The Big Heat

(William P. McGivern)

Probably it would be Estelle wanting to talk
of her predilection for the recondite
in matters sexual, in that insistent twang

of hers, or Tallulah—reputed flagellatrice—dialing to shock
him with her latest canard. No respite
for the leering but, as assuredly, no gang!

Whatever. It was eight o'clock
at night
when the phone rang.

Blood on the Moon

(James Ellroy)

I thought the demolition derby or
soapbox derby or a roller derby, anyway,
was where I would accompany my friend

Pilar. I thought we'd be out the door
when I mentioned "derby," but not on this day.
She just wanted to spend

the hours at home; join the antisocial corps,
maybe some quality time in the hay.
Before I could ascend

I figured it out: *Friday, June 10, 1964*
was the start of the KRLA
Golden Oldie weekend.

Stairway to an Empty Room

(Dolores Hitchens)

Horsefeathers! Monte was lost. His angst crested:
where was he really, and why? And before he was done
with this, wouldn't he long to know when? He tried

rearranging his thoughts. How he detested
the feeling that lingers after luncheon
with a menacingly addled

boss. The street had a peculiar arrested
quietness, as though everyone
on it had suddenly died.

A Graveyard to Let

(Carter Dickson)

The bright lights affected Carlene. "The estate
    of the enthralled is a lay too winsome to eschew,"
she opined, cavorting along the Great White Way.

She bore her fulsome Una Merkel perkiness straight
    to the stage, albeit a minor role in an antique tome few
could recall—replete with hope, anger, deceit, and dismay.

Not without reason did the late
    and great O. Henry refer to New
York as Bagdad-on-the-subway.

Downtown

(Ed McBain)

Dwight, the noted dour gourmand,
served his thin,
white soup. Mildred's committee

heard from swarthy and vagabond
Doctor Morales, their favorite drop-in
bon vivant. Thelma, pretty

song stylist, crooned and yawned
through some tunes from the '50s. (When
had lyricism been as giddy?)

Michael was telling the blonde
he'd never been
in this part of the city.

The Longest Second

(Bill S. Ballinger)

An extravaganza at
the Egyptian Theatre! Best double-bill
of the summer: *Saddle Tramp Death*

and *Wild Heritage*. We sat
in the loges, the expensive perspectives on Will
Rogers Jr. and Lizabeth

Scott. We'd come to see a little lariat
artistry, some fisticuffs, those polecats swill
their bourbon. As the footlights dimmed to Twentieth

Century Fox, our hearts froze. It can happen that
the planets stand still
and eternity holds its breath.

The Out Is Death

(Peter Rabe)

I asked myself—"Of all melancholy topics, what, according
to the universal understanding of mankind, is the most
melancholy! 'Death' was the obvious reply."
      —Edgar Allan Poe, *The Philosophy of Composition*, 1846

Through the Culver City cityscape
he trudged, rigid and ruly, toward
the Twentieth Century Club, briefcase

cuffed to his right wrist. To escape
he'd need to keep a quick eye, grip the bored
snubnose, his little pocket coup de grace.

What gives? One day the world's in your lap,
this puny existence its own reward;
then the next: Death's dog-mouthed grimace.

The tight overcoat gave him the long shape
of a tube and he walked bent forward
to keep the rain out of his face.

Blood of Poets

(Kenn Davis)

Poets who come to read their verse
Soon are riding in a hearse
    —copy from the front cover

In CA everyone wanted to be discovered,
even the poets. They'd ply their emotion
in the clubs; they'd persevere,
updating the varicose versified résumé . . .

They'd tell us: "like, luminous devils hovered,
dude, over Frisco," as if poetry were potion.
But let's face it: poetry is souvenir
and this is how it really was, day-to-day:

A fine mist covered
the city from the Pacific Ocean
beach to the piers
along the Embarcadero of the Bay.

City of Whispering Stone

(George C. Chesbro)

We all know men who flout
their demons, and men who—like us—
have none. But this! We'd dropped
into the "Russian Tea Room," half-assed

local parody in a building about
midway to the West Quad, to discuss
matters of less than grave import, adopt
the academic attitude and repast,

when I saw him. His new down-and-out
pose brought back all the unpleasantness;
he nodded from some spacey, repressed, chapped
demeanor. I kept my mouth shut; gazed, aghast.

My ex-boss looked uncomfortable and out
of place on the campus—
an unkempt genie who'd popped
without warning from the bottle of my past.

Judge Me Not

(John D. MacDonald)

She sat next to him on the bed. Blear-eyed,
groggy, he didn't recognize her. Couldn't keep
his peepers open . . . "the hell was this Jane Doe—

gussied in pink, reeking of talc—to hide—
what?" She stared down at him, her beauty skin deep
at least. Strains of La Rosa from the radio

in the dinette. He, still on this joyless joyride,
horizontal champion, victim of cheap-
thrill sedative, the ol' tongue-tied tableau.

When the woman left his side
he turned, in his sleep,
toward the window.

The Gentle Hangman

(James M. Fox)

A salesman at the marketplace
bedecked in a full Chicago and airtight

spiel. Local hoods in drag race
mode: that dog- and fistfight

of their Tulsa rolling stops, trace
narcotics. The town transvestite

festive in heels, Belgian lace,
parasol, eyebright,

and wrist tattoo of a hangman's noose
pulled tight.

The salesman winked. The pretty girl's face
was chalk white.

The Winter People

(Phyllis A. Whitney)

He said, *my life was a deep*
memory only, reflection of moon on a lake
in winter, then the snowing

for days. Like a key slipped to the lock of sleep
I'd rise just to measure time, to take
the news of it all, laughing.

I'd be on the town, pursuing cheap
pleasure or cheap pain; mistake
this lifetime for living.

It was like this: I was asleep
and then I was awake,
listening.

Invitation to Violence

(Lionel White)

Before the sword would compel
their devotion, was the fist mightier?
Did women of the cloth bargain

with the souls—au naturel—
of librarians? Was idle chatter
disruptive grace, or enabling stain?

What of the history of the feeble
gesture? De rigueur
contempt? Maledictive refrains?

Ignoring the legal
aspects of the matter,
the question still remains.

Deadline at Dawn

(William Irish)

Some dames give ya sob stories an' think
you're gonna purr . . .

Some give the ultimatum, and ya drink
till your blinkers and breath become a bleepin' blur . . .

Some dames'll kill ya with their celestial slink
and curvature . . .

But it ends. Like my pal said, "He was just a pink
dance-ticket to her."

Havana Run

(Les Standiford)

She'd run off with another Juan Doe;
I was, believe you me, sick of her flights.
All the anger I'd invested in her, daggone
it, had to add up to somethin'. Our cartoon

of a marriage: lotta grousing, just a lotta woe
to boot, but I'm not a guy who cools his heels. I got rights
and no Juan's gonna pull my leg. I packed a carry-on,
departed the Sun Palace and boarded the 9:49 from Cancun:

Midnight in Havana, the glow
of the ancient city's lights
curving above the distant horizon
like some pale, enormous moon.

Spend Game

(Jonathan Gash)

Miniature carnations, a something soufflé
—disguising a something a la king—
graced her table at the Mudflats Boatel.

She sipped the last of her chardonnay,
toyed, a moment, with her earring,
lamented the lack of anything subtle

in her life: an evening soiree,
a casual fling—
O to be half of an indiscreet couple!

No matter what people say,
you can't help getting
into trouble.

PREVIOUS POEMS

I.

The Sacred Cows of Los Angeles

Attention would-be bank robbers: this is a Spanish-speaking bank.
If you intend to rob us please be patient for we may need an interpreter.
—sign in the Banco de Paz, New York City

The Sacred Cows of Los Angeles

As if it had never happened
an old Angeleno will remember
the coming of the word *smog*.

How in 1948 a meteorologist
predicted the end of the past
in four letters. How the sacred

cows brought with them traffic
lights and street signs, cross
walks and the dotted line,

which after a while they began
to ignore. Pausing at corners,
they'd drool a pool of oil

and maybe etch a rubber patch,
leaving. They were fed
whatever it took. They were washed

and shined. At night they'd idle
through La Cienega or watch
from a lovers' lane over

the cool Pacific. They'd snooze
beneath the flickering face
of the Escondido Drive-In

or sleep in garages, nestled
in the waning fumes—safe,
a few hours, from the future, safe

the sight of the full moon,
a pomegranate resting
on the hazy lip of Los Angeles.

Snake

Because he lived
in one of those regions
where snake is the plural

of snake, when they told him
there were snake in his swamp
he understood. He did them in

with his shotgun. His daughter,
Magill, sometimes sobbed while
poling them out. The tears

in her eyes and the look in his:
a whole morning's religion—
and the corpse of snake

left be in the heat
not snake at all,
but several serpent.

"What Youngstown Needs Is Good Representation"

—Incumbent's election slogan

Let this represent Youngstown: Let
there be strangers taking the shade

on impossible verandas. Let them
be eating the dusk with the finest

of silver. Let them be decked out
in lobster bibs, with appropriate

manners, and plenty of melted butter
on hand. Let them sip civic pride

in the moonlight. Let them reflect
on their days in a concert of

various desserts. Let them retire
to discussions of the Department

of Public Works in their dreams.
Let an adequate darkness digest the

long hours of their sleep. Let
Youngstown be represented by this.

Introduction of the Shopping Cart

Oklahoma City, 1937

There was a man
who collected facts.

After work he rode twenty storeys,
let himself in
to cartons filled with index cards
and his crucial lists.

Facts reveal useful lives.
He got things right.

The shopping cart invented
by Sylvan Goldman,
Oklahoma City, 1937.

When the man passed on
his relatives came.

P. T. Barnum had four daughters.

They searched through his cartons
for ten-dollar bills.

The sky, which on cloudless
days appears to be azure,
has no true color.

He wasn't eccentric.
When they found nothing,
they threw everything
out.

His final fact:
you live and you die.

The shopping cart. P. T. Barnum.

The sky.

Houdini Disappearing in Philadelphia

Outside the theater
in his best bib and tucker,
we wondered where it was he went
once he'd reappeared.
Unlocked from that huge debris of chains
or risen from a trunk
bolted and submerged in a tank,
wouldn't he need a cold beer?

Wrists wringing with welts
as he held aloft the police handcuffs,
or loosed from a straightjacket
night after night in fifty seconds flat,
maybe he needed to escape.

Most likely it was to a new woman,
one to whom he could finally
and without fear
confess it all.

The man who could get out
of anything.
He disappeared into a cab
and headed off up Broad Street's
well-lighted and imaginable breach.

For Four Newsmen Murdered in Saigon

May, 1968

The sickening hush. Your auto
caught idle in the humid noon
with tires and windshield shot out
and surrounded by your riddled
bodies. These penalties for
point of view are accurate report

even in death. The street stinks
of terror and dust. In a moment
cowering refugees emerge from
hiding and quickly pass,
mumbling with stunned tongues
of watching you become the means

of your lost existence.
You might have been five dead—
but one, stumbling like a frightened
fawn at open fire, has feigned death
full account and lived
to tell us how it is trying to tell
us how it is.

Newlywed

The newlyweds
never watch closely

enough. The way the
preacher's appropriate

solemnity astounds them.
The way the best man

picks up the tab and slips
off into the receiving

line. There is something
to be said

for his rented
tuxedo, and the laps

of the bridesmaids are
no less luxurious.

The way the groom's
spinster sister sighs. The

way the guests, recognizing
an honorable intention

when they see one,
weep.

Badlands

In the midst of the badlands
cowboys sipping coffee from
tin cups squat around a fire.

An organ-grinder moves among
them, his monkey soliciting
grub. Their horses are poker-

faced and even the cowboys
grow stoic. They pretend they
imagine all this. Smoke from

their fire pirouettes toward the
moon. Cattle are everywhere
seeking spring range. The organ-

grinder farts. The monkey
chuckles, and the cowboys chew
their platitudes just like on TV.

The Resurrection of Lake Erie

Everything before me turns to allegory
—Jose Emilio Pacheco

Soon after the word went out,
dismembered bodies cast off
in barrels by the mafiosi

fused, and hatching from those eggs
of slat, swam toward
the shore of the new life.

The rotting fish righted themselves
and went on. Plant life again.
And clear, warm breezes

moved through Cleveland, Dunkirk,
and Buffalo. In the air, geese,
their honking and a pleasure

in the sadness of natural life—
its second chance.
From the beaches the waving arms

of bathers signaled the freighters,
signaled the sloop cutting across
to Port Stanley.

Dinosaurs of the Hollywood Delta

Joe DiMaggio, who was married for three years to Marilyn Monroe, has ended
a 20-year standing order for thrice-weekly delivery of roses to her crypt.
The florist said Mr. DiMaggio gave no explanation.
—*The New York Times*, September 30, 1982

In times of plenty
they arrived from everywhere
to forage among the palmettos
of Beverly and Vine, to roam
the soda fountains and dime stores
of paradise. For every Miss Tupelo

who got a break, whose blonde
tresses made it to the silver screen,
whose studio sent her on a whirlwind
tour to Chicago, and to the Roxy
in Manhattan where she'd chat
with an audience, do a little tap

dance, and answer questions
about the morality of the jitterbug,
thousands became extinct.
Their beauty, it was said, drove
men to wallow in dark
booths in the Florentine

Lounge, dreaming of voluptuous
vanilla, though the rumor persists
that they were dumb.

They were called *Jean, Rita, Jayne,*
Mae, and Betty. The easy names.

No one remembers now
how the waning of their kind
began. Theories have pointed
to our own growing sophistication—
as if that were a part of natural
selection. At first we missed
them little, and only in that detached

manner one laments the passing
of any passing thing. Then posters
began to appear. Whole boutiques
adoring their fashion: heavy rouge,
thick lipstick. The sensuous puckering
of lips. Surreptitious giggling.

We began to congregate on street corners
at night, Santa Monica and La Brea,
to erect searchlights
and marquees announcing premieres
for which there were no films.
We looked upward

as if what had been taken from us
were somehow etched in starlight above
their sacred city. We began
to chant, demanding their return—
to learn, for once, the meaning
of their desperate, flagrant love.

II.

Living the Good Life on the San Andreas Fault

Living the Good Life on the San Andreas Fault

Every day in Daly City
is part of the beginning
of the end. There at the tip

where the great fault
runs from Mexico to lose
itself in the sea,

they wait for the one morning
when they will slide faster
than they do now

toward watery graves
beneath the Aleutians. How
the fiery night will extinguish

itself where the earth opens
to feed on its own tender
crust! For a hundred years

they will be the news
that diminishes slowly to
a simple lesson: *there is just*

cause for misgiving. Not all
our worry is needless.
This is the price they pay

for living the good life.
The price for the freedom
of extravagant loving, the food

and the cars. For the abundance
of mesmerization, the making it,
and the overlooked bountiful

losing. For the guilt. The price
they want to pay for living
in the midst of an enchantment

called America
which like every fairy tale

needs its wicked witch.

The Problems, the Models

Let us build models of our problems that
we might visualize them clearly.
—from a Sunday morning religious program

Let us build models
of our problems that we

might visualize them
clearly. Let them tower

above us the way Grief
looms over a widow. Let

us determine what we can
see in the beautifully

tormenting eyes of Agony.
Let us learn firsthand

that Anxiety has a wart
on her nose, that as

a fact of her life
she despises children as

much as adults. Let us
know once and for all

that wherever we are
one of the eight faces

of Despair is always on
our side.

The Riot of Nickel Beer Night

While the Red Sox were taking it
on the chin from the Twins,
and the Orioles were blowing
another big lead to the Yankees,
in the bottom of the ninth

in Cleveland some fan jumped
out of the stands and punched Jeff
Burroughs in the nose.
The customers in the right field
seats, not satisfied

by anything, not by the fireworks
and the smoke bombs,
not the ball game, not
by even this dream of three
hours of cheap beer, joined in.

For a bruiser like Burroughs
it was a defeat
he could stare in the face
and understand. He made
for the dugout as they flocked

after him. Afterwards the ump,
Nestor Chylak, forfeited it
to the Rangers. Nursing the bump
on his skull broached by an airborne
bottle, he told reporters

the fans stunk up the place—
the place was a zoo.
So it was no joke when, for days
after, the replay
from the center field camera

showed us those fans swarming
toward home plate like mobs of angry
birds inexplicably drawn
to the entrance
of a narrow tunnel

and, while the announcer
mumbled something about the modern
era, in the foreground the one
small boy,
sober and disinterested

in fisticuffs
but grateful for a chance
on the surface of the big time,
turning cartwheels across
the outfield.

Manhattan As a Latin American Capital

How can this be happening in the Palace
of Justice? Senators,
Judges in their seasonal robes
fleeing through the burning colonnades!
Captains of industry escaping
in tinted limousines; the dictators
of fashion unheard from for weeks.
A Broadway of sawdust, dead poultry.
Guerrillas slowly metabolizing
the culture. Scattered resistance
in the Garment District. In the galleries
death squads, in the name of posterity,
machine-gunning, amigos,
all the precious art.

In the Aviary

High above you some fool
in a biplane is seeding
the clouds. You curse him
aloud. You threaten him
with the flak of your fists.
Farther along, three
archetypal owls out on a
limb begin hooting at you.
You pelt them with small
stones, consistently missing.
A parrot from the bushes
calls you a fly-by-night
something-or-other, and two
snowy egrets cough soot
on your shoes.
Deeper into the beautiful
garden, vultures circle your
heart like apostles of grief
marking time.

Nobody Lives on Arthur Godfrey Boulevard

When I first heard about America
it was already too late. When I learned
that its holiest city is Dallas,
Texas, there was nothing I could do
but bear witness to the deckled edge

of Manifest Destiny, California
well on its way to becoming
an island, or some foreign country
where one of the many forms
of English is still spoken.

I had missed the arduous construction
of democracy, though I lived among
its numbered days. What I saw
was the Reconstruction of Fifth Avenue,
and the Army Corps of Engineers

dredging sand from the sea
and piling it back where the beaches
belong. I heard wry assemblages
of Rotarians, Shriners, and Optimists,
Elks and Moose committing business

over lunch. I listened as
my friends wondered at the poverty
that affluence breeds,
not quite believing in the life
lived on Frank Sinatra Drive,

nor in the one where nobody lives
on Arthur Godfrey Boulevard. I watched
brotherhood practiced among corporations,
and freedom in the emporiums
of fast food. The separation of church

and religion. I saw all of us
becoming stranded everywhere
in our land, the new Pilgrims arrived
at last on the shore of a great
desert, mouthing our own sad psalms.

III.

At Irony's Picnic

The Rise of the Sunday School Movement

I am not a healer. Jesus is the healer.
I am only the little girl who opens the door
and says "Come in."
  —Aimee Semple McPherson

I had wanted my daughter
to become an evangelist—
Sister Lizabeth Adrienne, say—
not to relive my life in hers,
nor for desire after the great abstraction

in lieu of the bits of carpentry
I've managed. No, like anyone
I just longed for a little pomp amid
all of this circumstance.
A progeny who could shout *Sweet*

Beautiful Jesus and mean it.
To have borne
a pillar in the rise
of the Sunday School Movement,
or one of the overdue

Northern Crusades. One who could
espy the dance halls of Venice,
California, with the true conviction
of a Sunday afternoon; who could bathe
in the sea at Carmel and not

disappear for three weeks
in Mexico with her married lover;
who'd never be transported
back from the lost, paraded
in a throne of white

wicker from her private train car
to overdose on tablets
of the newest redemption.
The way I figured it,
I'd be sitting at a corner table

in the Desdemona Club
nursing a brew. She'd be up
there on the large-screen TV next
to the bar, having taken over Billy
Graham's Asian Tour after his terrible

swift heart attack in China. The petite
brunette beauty from America!
She'd be singing "Lord,
We Need Thee Every Hour" as
the afflicted clutched at the hem

of her flowing dress. Maybe
I'd kneel among them, then
and there. Begin
to believe as we're able to believe
what reaches us by satellite—

bow down as she gave us
the beauteous word, all of us praising,
loving her, adoring the celestial
melody, possessed by our irrevocable
conversions.

Braille

The blind folding their dollar
bills in half. Giving the fives
a crease on each corner; leaving
the tens smooth as a knuckle.

There are ways, even in trust
among the rank and file of the seeing,
not to be bilked.

The blind leading the blind
is not so bad—

how it is lost on us every day
that you can learn all
of the world you need to know
by tapping it gently
with a stick.

Grasshoppers

Atomic radiation gets the blame again as monster
grasshoppers make a shambles of Illinois.
    —TV *Guide*

Suddenly they appeared,
addicts for everything in
Illinois. They removed
Peoria in a minute, the populace
drowning in a liquid with the
sharp odor of tobacco juice.
In Carbondale
grasshopper eyes were seen in the
distance, luminous as astronauts'
visors. Then came the end. Chicago's
buildings were crushed in a holocaust
of mandibles. They scuttled
Skokie. Moline was a maelstrom
as they moved toward the borders
where, in the face of signs reading
Welcome to Indiana, Kentucky, Missouri,
Iowa, and Wisconsin, they collapsed dying
to their gargantuan knees.

Flagpole Sitter

Remember? I perched
atop those flagless
poles of the fifties
and waited. This

was at carnivals,
grand openings of gas
stations, and state
centennials. I was

up there with my summer
cold like a kid hiding
in his tree house from
Mom. You waved

when you passed, wondering
why I did it. When I
broke the record I came
down and slept for

weeks. I was all the
rage then. But I
knew no fame or any reason
for my act; only

as with a man who keeps both
feet on the
ground, the alleged
fact of time.

Seeing My Name in *TV Guide*

It was there, early Sunday
morning, in the Seattle Edition.
I was the writer on the arts

program reading selections
from his recent book,
opposite a wild party causes

a teenage girl to question her
values, a run-in with the school
principal teaches Davey

that God is approachable, and Ronald
Reagan in good form as an ex-marshal
who has to clean up a lawless town

before he can settle down.
In the next hour *Insight* focused
on the National Conscience,

Uncle Joe fell for a visiting
librarian, Tippi Hedren
discussed her pets.

Hunger

An owl shuffles
in the cold eye of

the moon. In low
ground blind mice

are alive. Even hunger
is as old as these hills

where everything known
is a risk. What can we

learn from the dangers
of this world,

like driving through
mountains in rain—

from loving and later
like orphans of night

from trekking the slow
depths of sleep?

A Tax Auditor for the IRS Dreams

Who was the previous owner
of your moustache? Have

you ever been intimate
with either of the Baker

sisters of Clovis, New Mexico?
Do you see any relation

between wallabies and blue-
collar humor? Do you often

think of death or airplanes
as the only way out? Have you

ever blamed anything on
the bossa nova?

What's that quarter doing
on the piano?

At Irony's Picnic

Silence is sight-reading
Swahili. Sin lumbers by on

stilts. Where did he get
that Hawaiian shirt? Those

rose-colored glasses? Down
by the lake Desire is fondling

Regret's mother. Jealousy
And Happiness dance the mazurka.

Justice, wearing the same
old swimsuit, is cutting the

ballyhoo. Irony himself
isn't even here.

IV.

Bournehurst-on-the-Canal

Landscape with Unemployed Jockeys

It was a landscape
with unemployed jockeys,
a landscape of rubric
and confection.
One could imagine
the outskirts of Louisville
and from there, who knows?—
the fringes of Tulsa
and on along the power
lines to Blanche Laborde, Queen
of Long Beach, crooning
"Love Me With All Your Heart";
the theatrics of Darius
Lawrence or Bertha
Lammell. It was a landscape
wherein the boots
were spiffed and shined,
and the riding breeches held up
with suspenders. A landscape
of dejection and fluency,
of idle tack.
It was a landscape
with unemployed jockeys,
the colors of their silks
dazzling and littering
the hillsides and nothing
doing at the downs.

The Bigamist

He lives to learn
the loopholes in his
speech,
the way the easy journey
from Memphis to Mobile
makes him forget
one-half of everything.
Darlings, as sure
as there are two of
you, there are two of him
walking among us
somewhere, disguised
in his accustomed
civilian clothes.

Everything You Own

Sometimes I think you're
from the South. You speak

with that drawl. You move
slowly as if taken by heat.

There are burning desires,
strange elevations you

never overcome. Everything
you own is in your

pockets. I see you in the
drugstore down on Main,

sipping soda, spitting
tobacco, mopping your brow.

You could tell me what this
country needs.

Stargazers

In memory of Frank Stanford

Whoever predicted the silver Cadillac
parked in the lot,
that fez of an American
potentate left behind on the seat,
whoever diverted words
like *mercurial* into the horoscopes and
foretold croupiers bent
over gaming tables
in the half light, offering
the beginning of religion again,
whoever felt the constant movement
of even the farthest stars
as they bruise the air we breathe
could decipher a farmer
standing deep in his field
swatting the flies from his face,
the press agent visiting his daughter
in Des Moines,
or *a fat lady in a housecoat*
walking through rooms with a cage,
calling a bird.

Five Small Songs of America in 2076

1.

It will finally be admitted
in medical circles
that everything
causes cancer in white
mice.

2.

They will sell tickets
to the cloning
of the cloning of Mick
Jagger.

3.

There will be accusations
of planned obsolescence
in the manufacture
of artificial
hearts.

4.

Think of capitalism
as the chic
nostalgia.

5.

Even then
they'll be dreaming
of the future.

Carl Yastrzemski

Harwich, Massachusetts, 1981

When the bratty kids
followed me out of the ballpark
demanding my autograph,
I told them they had the wrong guy.

   Yaz lived in our summer
town, while his college boy played
for the local team. He'd been seen
seldom and so, like every hero,
remained larger than life but smaller
than rumor. These ruffians
wanted his signature and what
could I do in the minute I wasn't him
and only I knew it.

       When they grabbed
at my windbreaker and went
for my BoSox cap, I sprinted
through the parking lot
and into the car just as Yaz
must have done that first time
he'd driven off, heart pounding,
a real American night the diminishing
radius of his anonymity.

At home,
my wife and children asleep,
everything locked up, I sat in the low
light of the study. Oh, I'd played ball
in my day all right. Whiffed against
Little Leaguers who later made the Majors,
who in our 29th year were referred
to as *veterans*, while I received lesser
acclaim for being young at what I do.

As sometimes happens,
I began to write it down.
Not this, but something like it
about falling beneath a knockdown pitch
just in time. Getting up and digging in,
and busting a high hard one out of sight
when maybe the real story was just
a misunderstanding with the boss
or an article in the *Times* about Frankie
Lymon's widows.

I did this night after night
with the dedication of Yaz
and the consolation of nobody
wanting the real me to sign anything. Alone,
tapping the plate before thousands of fans,
swinging for the fences with the childhood
of Johnny Carson or a television memory
of the Dalai Lama. Stroking line drives
with nothing in my hands but Aristophanes
on *the bitterness of figs*.

Year after
year, with no Ford dealership
for the off-season, without a big contract
or hope for arbitration. Over
and over I'd do it, not for the fame,
god, not for the money,
but for what darker, sweeter
compensation?

Vigilantes

There was a time in
their country when they
patrolled the streets
of villages on horseback,
lynching murderers and
thieves at gatherings
so formal they called them
necktie parties.

They wore sure thin smiles
as they yoked violence
from shadows to the
light.

When law broke down in
their towns they bent over it
and looked with pity deep into
its giant eyes. They offered
it smelling salts and soothed its
wounds. They stroked it,
they picked it up, they took it
into their own hands.

The Man Who Invented Las Vegas

In church he never felt
the weight of God, which
hangs in those places heavier

than any mist; he felt only
the overwhelming presence of
luck. When he knelt, his bones

cracked like loaded dice
and fell into place. The choirs
he heard were of roulette wheels

spinning in rooms velvet
and vacant of light as an altar
without candles. He saw

middle-aged housewives
grown tired of marriages more
sour than lemons standing in rows,

pulling the levers of slot
machines again and again, often
not seeing the final combinations

of their unexotic fruit. The
fascinations of boredom and
chance! He gathered electricity

and with its flashes and spurts
and steady rays turned darkness
out of the desert forever
thinking *we shall never sleep.*
He witnessed the spectacle
from a distance, and in

the trance of a child staring
into his first fire,
learning the beauty and heat

of its rage. And he thought not
that it was good or bad,
but that what he had made

was a thing some of the people
who live on earth for a while
could believe in.

When Guy Lombardo Died

New Year's Eve went
with him. On December 31

all of the people on the
earth's dark face

forgot how to dance.
Days later when they remembered

to Foxtrot, there was no
need. In the minute of midnight

gravity was suspended. The ball
atop the Times Square building

refused to descend. For the
first time rain swirled

unimpeded by bodies
to the pavement of those streets, the

air a vacancy of kisses and
noisemakers. In the morning

people came from their houses
with no hangovers, and stone sober

proceeded with the old business
of the world.

In the Blood

Vodka is the aunt of wine
   —Russian proverb

Money is the rich
uncle of parliamentary
procedure. Impropriety
the handmaiden of desire.
Lust is a skeleton
in the closet of love,
and horsewhips are the fathers
of no questions asked.
The waddle is kin
to the walk. Virtue is that
wallflower cousin of vice.
Charity is related to no one,
though the monocle
is half brother to the spectacles
and water is just the looser
sister of ice.

Bournehurst-on-the-Canal

They arrive in the blustery
summer twilight, couples in coupes,
roadsters, and touring cars, up

from Falmouth and Hyannisport
in Palm Beach suits and taffeta weave.
There is dancing to Paul Whiteman

and Alice Fay. What summons
our attention—my mother-in-law told
me this—is not the soft flags luffing

at each high corner of the pavilion,
nor the placards for photoplays screened
—during the week and after the season—

on the lower level. Not the darkened
interior, the bandstand surrounded
by potted ferns and huge portal

archways, those boxed lights
with dim figures of dancing goddesses
suspended from the iron

mesh ceiling. Never mind
that all of this will burn to the cliffside
in the autumn of 1933. Tonight it is

the one couple, vaguely familiar, lingering
by the path. They are having a quarrel—
over sex or money, because what else

could it be? Never mind that within thirty
years their eldest daughter will be
a school marm in another part

of the state; that their youngest,
surely the more beautiful and promising,
will have entered into an arrangement

with the Rathbone sisters
which will be marked by sadness
and disappointment. Never mind that their

only son, a graduate of Colby College,
will live in Cleveland and embark
on a livelihood seldom

mentioned at family gatherings. Tonight
they are young and are having
a quarrel. It is one of those evenings

full of such stirrings as only memory
will adequately "take into account." Just now
the orchestra strikes up and music

floats over the distance to where they are
being a little brusque with each other,
a little stubborn.

And now, as if called, they begin to move
toward the ballroom entrance, he slightly ahead
and tugging at her wrist, though not quite

so much to cause pain.
He believes the moment has passed
and he is leading her toward

an evening of happiness.
Toward a lifetime
of happiness.

V.

Washington Park

Death was process then, a release of nostalgia
    Leaving you free to change.
Perhaps you were wrong; but walking at night
    Each house got personal. Each
Had a father. He was reading a story so hopeless,
    So starless, we all belonged.
        —Jon Anderson

Near Lacombe

Fastened to his rocker,
the old man rocked for hours
making stories from his life.
We heard his watch ticking
on its chain and smelled
the odor of his pipe
across the dusty room.

What we heard was
how hard it had been at first,
coming West—
how he'd been the one who helped
discover oil near Rimbey
making instant promise of the place—
how his good wife had loved these
lonely hours clean till her death.

And what we heard was
nothing
of what he thought he'd said.

Building

My grandfather was a builder
who sweat words into stone
then blasted with hammer
and nails his plans toward form.

His was a poetry of concrete
made poetry by his hands—
though he told me once

before driving to work,
when his heart exploded him
off the road,

that he'd often wished his
several selves, strangers that
they seemed,
might have fit better
into his wrinkling skin.

My Kindergarten Girlfriend

My kindergarten girl friend
had fat cheeks and chubby legs
but she was sweet. My thoughts
were of pulling up her dress;
not kissing in the coat closet
or grabbing her ponytail.

I imagine she's married now. I
see her husband harried at breakfast,
belching yolks of eggs she's slung
and swizzling his hot coffee.
She stands there in her tattered
robe, hair in pin clips, scowling.
He looks up and says

ya know, you used to didn't be
a bad lookin' woman.

Pastoral

Lambs are gamboling
on the lawn. The goat

is chewing a tire off
the '39 Dodge. I notice

the faces of the sky
keep returning.

I think: Out here we
find ourselves by losing

others. Just then my
father steps through

the trees, carrying ambition
like an armload of leaves.

The Old Neighborhood

There was a time in my life when,
each evening after work,
I'd go down and sit in the bowling
alley. It was the only place

I could feel superior then,
watching the men in their leisure
suits and the funny shoes,
their fluffy-honey wives in toreadors

who always needed a few more
pointers just to get it wrong again.
I began to learn the strange
power that comes of watching well:

I knew the exhilaration in a mounting
score for Flo's Boutique or Genuine
Auto Parts. I wanted for myself
these simple feats destined

to be the life of the next beer
blast. I began to want something
funny to tell the guys down
at some plant—

instead of only the wondering
at how things happen, at how
people I loved and people I didn't
crept up on me even while

I was paying attention,
at how I'd come to be sitting
night after night
between the soda fountain

and the scorers' benches,
unwelcome in the old
neighborhood
once more.

Potatoes

Grandpa said potatoes
reminded him of school.

Potatoes and school.
He said he'd wake nearly

freezing, kindle a fire
and throw two potatoes

on. Going to school
he carried them to

warm his hands. To
warm his feet he ran.

He said by noontime
those potatoes almost

froze; said he ate a lot
of cold potatoes for lunch.

Toward San Francisco

We come here to forget
the ash-damp summer Boston,
a baby daughter who should have been.
Five days across the scorching land,
still all our thoughts,
our sparse words are interrogative.
Exchanging Spock for guidebook and map
we accept what direction we can get
for two turned tourists
once so well prepared for parenthood.

Heading into the Sierras past sunset
a cool breeze soothes the wound
that time will heal.
I watch your sleeping face
scarred far too old
wince in the wind . . .
and I drive on, dreading another night
spent apart from myself.

Jungles

If nothing between you
and this world was right,
you never said as much.

One day, without leaving,
you simply retreated to
seek your fortune

as if some California still
existed, as if it were a state
of mind. You learned

the rootlessness within
the body makes that journey
difficult.

Those letters to your
loved one in Pennsylvania
from whichever remote

village inside yourself
you sent them
told her of nothing but your

exquisite and declining
penmanship. Years later,
informed of your death

I think of all the time
we spend probing the dark
continents of ourselves,

of what happens when a man
at last, unshaven and ill-kempt
walks out of the jungles

of his own heart
carrying not even so much
as an answer.

Washington Park

I went walking in the Rose Gardens.
It was about to rain, but the roses
were beginning to bloom. The Olympiads,

some Shreveports, and the Royal
Sunsets. This was in the beautiful
city I had taken away from myself

years before, and now I was giving it back.
I walked over the Rosaria tiles
and found Queen Joan of 1945. I sat

on the hillside overlooking the reservoir
and studied the Willamette and the Douglas
firs. I learned the traffic

and the new high-rises as the rain
came down.
This leaving and returning,

years of anger and forgiveness,
the attempts to forgive one's self—
it's everybody's story

and I was sitting there
filling up again with the part of it
that was mine.

VI.

What's Wrong with the Moon?

What's Wrong with the Moon?

1.

Sue Baseball? No Kid, that would be like suing the Church!
—William Bendix in *The Babe Ruth Story*

I first chose language because I needed a weapon with which to defend myself. As far as I knew it had no cost and it was legal. I grew up, like most boys my age, wanting a life of athletics. Nothing unusual in that. The expectation of becoming a hero, of achieving fame perhaps. Maybe just being accomplished at something we enjoyed doing. To that end we taught ourselves what we thought America wanted us to learn: determination, fair play, dedication to a craft, the honing of mental and physical skills, that perseverance offsets a lack of natural ability, the (always undelineated) virtue of competition, and the most elusive of achievements, patience in all of this. Despite some moderate early success, it was a dream that ended soon enough. Lack of size, speed, talent. The need to earn a living. There are few compensations.

I was born in the state of Oregon, and I often lament that it has not been my lot to have spent my adult years there. Its natural beauty is astounding. The Pacific coast. The rivers and forests and snowcapped mountains. I fished and rafted, spent summers in my grandparents' bungalow overlooking the ocean at Cannon Beach, and in winter climbed Mount Hood with the Mazamas. But there was an ogre in paradise. I was an abused child. For more than ten years every hour spent away from home was a reprieve. I excelled in school. I was the only one in my class who luxuriated in the major requirement of the era, reading *Silas Marner*. I excelled at games. I excelled at observing and appreciating the Great Northwest. How could it have been that my excellence vanished whenever I entered my own house? Despite my mother's tireless efforts, my brothers and I were part of what is now called a "dysfunctional family." Lives go wrong. Very early I took to spending the hours at home inventing scenes and stories. I wrote them down. Little autobiographical forgeries. I succeeded in each of them, and they were my salvation. Their requirements were few. They had to be literal enough for understanding, and so clearly stated that I could believe them. A concocted life of comfort. I suppose, with all one hears about child abuse these days, I was extremely lucky, and this activity was the best that could come of that sad condition.

2.

Obviously I don't recommend the way I came to writing to anyone. And once it became an established part of my life I wish I could say it had caused me no anguish or suffering. Writing has been a source of satisfaction and vulnerability, of accomplishment and self-doubt. If a writer's standards become more demanding along the way, as I believe they should, he cannot avoid a feeling of helplessness: the discrepancy between what he is able to write and that which he will accept as good writing. Completing a poem is, in part, an unsettling proposition. One never knows if he'll ever write another.

I can say there were excellent teachers in the schools I attended. Strict grammarians and people who loved literature. People who gave advice and support. Two of them taught creative writing in high school—curriculum subject unheard of then. One teacher, dramatic and writerly, informed us by demonstration; the other simply asked us to write a great deal and had important things to say about everything we wrote. I can say there are worlds to be gained in attending a college such as Harvard. I wish I'd had a lifetime to spend as a student there, though as an aspiring writer then, I remain a bit disappointed that the place had not seen fit in matters literary "to enquire into the twentieth century" yet. Grateful as I am for the background in the tradition of poetry the exercises provided me, I believe I wrote all the sonnets and heroic couplets there I will ever need to write. Then the liberation of the Writing Seminars at Johns Hopkins, where in the late 1960s we read Donald Barthelme and translations of Pablo Neruda and listened to Robert Bly and Allen Ginsberg! The longtime director there, more a friend than we deserved, who showed us that, much as we wanted not to believe it, writing would never be a communal endeavor. It was the beginning of "survival without being a member of the club." And the generous colleague in the design department at Carnegie Mellon who taught me how to publish books by others, though it takes a long time to learn to serve poetry well.

These are the facts, a little tainted by opinion.

3.

Writers who claim never to read reviews of their work and to pay no attention to critics have to be kidding. I've been flattered by praise and stung (and yes, helped) by criticism. My poems have been called "comic" and "humorous" and "funny" and "witty" and "satirical" and work that has its base in "American pseudo-philosophy." One writer even called them "serious," and she's the one I believe. I think they are about the most serious things I know. A reviewer of *In the Aviary* put it this way: "He is at once the lecturer at the podium and the delinquent asleep at the back of the hall." Yes, that's what I was after. Is that position a comic one, or a tragic?

4.

The certainty of place, the certainty that we are not lost, the
certainty that the world and our lives have checkpoints with
names and definite directions that we can follow, the certainty.
    —Richard Hugo in *The Real West Marginal Way*

In 1945, the year I was born, there were about 139 million people living
in the United States. The most recent census has confirmed the current
population at more than 320 million. How is it that optimism persists?
Who could fail to understand the profound meaning such numbers have
for the way we are able to live?

If there were fewer of us then, it is also true that we were more regional.
Television had yet to "homogenize" America. I saw television for the first
time when I was seven. Before then it was radio and the great imagining that
I loved; the scenes that every program forced us to produce for ourselves. I
spent summer nights on the Oregon coast tuning in whatever I could pick
up: Seattle, Coos Bay, and Oakland. The mystique of place. I could imagine
San Francisco and Hollywood! Later, I studied maps in order to locate them
precisely. I became intoxicated by the sounds of their names: Scappoose,
Walla Walla. They were places of hundreds of plausible "other" lives. The
certainty. I could imagine everything.

5.

The *Oxford English Dictionary* describes the adjective "comic" by employing the words "trivial" and "fortunate."

6.

The events of our early, "formative" years continue to shape the ways we feel about ourselves. They shape a writer's "vision" of the world and, consequently, the manner in which that vision is articulated. Doubtless there are "therapists" who are convinced they can free us from the past, or at least help us to "come to terms" with it. But, sixty years later, I feel about my life little differently than I did when I was five: no matter how it is going at the moment, it's a burden. And writing remains a means for managing that. It's a matter of specific events and how we feel about them.

I must have been about six when my grandfather took me to visit the Indians at Celilo Falls. Their village was situated on the banks of the Columbia River just east of The Dalles, Oregon. We always referred to them as the Celilo Indians, though actually they were a small community consisting of members of the Umatilla, Yakama, Warm Springs, and Nez Perce tribes. Because of the diminishing numbers among these tribes by the 1940s, it was inevitable that they live together, and possible, one of them told me, because of the similarity of their native languages. They lived in tepees, and we used to watch them net salmon from the precarious scaffolding they had erected out over the falls that fell in three directions at that section of the river.

In the early 1950s, the government, interested in "bettering their lot," razed the tepees and constructed a new outpost of prefabricated houses. Within six months the Indians had removed the housing and reconstructed their tepees around the indoor plumbing.

The increasing need in the West for electric power brought about the construction of The Dalles Dam, which was completed in 1957. The entire town of Biggs (in close proximity to the village at Celilo, and the boyhood home of one Doc Severinsen, bandleader on the *Tonight Show* with Johnny Carson) was carefully dismantled and moved up the mountain where it was reassembled intact. But the backwaters covered Celilo. The villagers were removed to the Warms Springs Indian Reservation one hundred miles to the south. As I remember, there was litigation, and the powers that be "sat on their hands" for as long as possible. By 1963, the year I graduated from high school, the checks had gone out. In the second semester one of my classmates began driving a new Corvette to school each day—conspicuous in that time and place. The story went that she was one-sixteenth Indian and had received the sum of $20,000 from the U.S. government for inconvenience to her race.

Today a state park commemorates Celilo. Adjacent to it is Celilo Village, a place of twenty-odd prefabricated houses built for those who insisted on returning from the Warm Springs Reservation to live out their lives near the river. The villagers hosted a picnic recently, inviting me and anyone who remembered them to come and reminisce.

7.

What could be more deeply perplexing than leading an existence that, day to day, is marked by a combination of pathetic and humorous elements?

8.

It is only in fairy tales that anyone actually finds a needle in a haystack.
—Heinrich Boll

I had taken my first job and we were moving to a new city. I wanted to be a writer and the furniture haulers had damaged my typewriter, so you know what that meant. The first Monday found me in the local corporate headquarters and repair shop of one of our nation's leading manufacturers of office equipment. I hoisted my machine onto the counter.

"How much will this be?" I asked. "To fix the carriage return." The short, mustachioed fellow, without a word, nodded toward a sign directly over my head that read "$25 Minimum Charge on All Work."

"That's just for the estimate," he said. "After that it's parts and labor."

"Kind of steep, isn't it?" I asked.

"Well," he smiled, "last week it was $15, but IBM raised their prices and in order to remain competitive, we had to raise ours too."

Every social studies and civics class I'd ever taken said this wasn't so. I remembered arguing endlessly with the foreign exchange student from Portugal who preached the evils of capitalism. He saw competition as a wasteful duplication of effort. All those competing dairies who sent their milk trucks through our neighborhoods, wasting the gasoline and the human resources to leave glass bottles by our doorsteps. He was proud that his town was served by a single truck. The logic that his truck could ask any amount it wanted for its bottles was lost on him. And suddenly it was lost on me.

"It's just a broken spring," I said. "A little shorter than your fingernail. I can see it in there. How much for one of those?"

He looked it up.

"It's seven cents, but I gotta charge you more." He pointed to another sign hanging above the bench that read "Minimum Charge $10 for All Parts."

"You're going to charge me $10 for a seven-cent spring," I stated. And then, despite my usual even-tempered nature, I began to shout. Immediately thereafter a tall man in a flowered tie pushed through the swinging doors and inquired about "all the commotion." The mustache explained it to him, and the tie proceeded to a small chest about the size of a tackle box where he dipped his tongs into one of the tiny drawers, pulled out a silver spring, and slipped it neatly into one of those teeny manila envelopes the dentist gives you to take your extracted teeth home in.

Reaching to hand it to me, he said: "And now I trust we shall never see you again."

All afternoon I worked at it, tears of frustration welling up. With an assortment of screwdrivers, with pliers both common and needle-nose, with my wife's tweezers, with mirrors. For America. For myself. I fixed it.

9.

Happy endings are defined by abbreviated lives.

10.

We were in the car. My daughter, ten, up front. My son, seven, in back. It was after dark and we were driving home. That writing is one of my continuing activities is something I had never discussed with my children. So it was with more than a little innocence that she interrupted the reverie of that spring evening to announce she had written a poem about the moon and wished (her word) to recite it to us. And then the surprising high-pitched laughter from the backseat that filled the car. Chipmunk convulsion. That little grade-school male hatred of poetry that most of us carry with us always. Call it the misunderstanding. But one certain in its derision. The incredulity that anyone would admit to poetry, let alone wanting to write or perform it. His mirth seemed inexhaustible, and, taken by the intensity of the laughter, its sound, the normalcy, the beauty of its naïveté, I too began to laugh.

I saw her nostrils widen. What could I say? Some things are too subtle—even for a father who loves words—to explain to a daughter in such circumstances. When she had finally had enough, she enunciated slowly and with only slight trembling, "WHAT'S WRONG WITH THE MOON? All you ever write about is Arthur Godfrey!"

11.

There is less that distinguishes comedy from tragedy than is generally
believed.

12.

My children were raised in one of those "bedroom communities" so theoretically perfect that its design included a system of elementary schools within walking distance of every home. Something about entitlement. They could come home for lunch! On one of those autumn days in my daughter's tenth year, she entered the kitchen, poured herself a glass of milk, and proceeded to the dining room where the day's mail, spread out across the table, included copies of a new magazine that contained two of my poems. From the living room, I saw her open the journal with great care and begin to read, though not for more than five seconds, when her mother called her to her sandwich. She placed the issue back on the table and returned to the kitchen. Suddenly aware that I had been watching, she blurted out, "It's pretty good, Dad. So far."

13.

Cloudy with showers

—weather forecast for Portland, Oregon, October 12, 1962

On Columbus Day 1962, we experienced the greatest natural disaster to occur on the West Coast since the San Francisco earthquake of 1906. It was a Friday, the day of the game against Beaverton. Our new football coach, Mouse Davis, had installed the rudiments of what has become the run-and-shoot offense, and we were having a terrific season with only a single four-point loss on our record. It was my senior year, and I was having fun playing quarterback in a system where intelligence counted as much as brawn. I had made application to the University of Chicago, Harvard, and Brown and had just received a letter from the Brown coach "wishing me luck in what just might be the championship" game. I was living on high hopes.

It had been a day of listlessness at school. At home, afterwards, waiting for Randy Burchfield, one of my teammates, to pick me up, the sun began to shine. An eerie late afternoon light. Shortly before he arrived, the wind began to blow. In the distance of nearly three blocks between our house and the traffic light where we entered the main road, we were forced to stop twice to remove fallen branches in order to proceed. We thought little of it. Burchfield moved through the light, which was swinging wildly, and drove, buffeted by wind and the debris of leaves, branches, and articles of clothing, the four miles to the high school. We strode to the locker room, packed our gear, and boarded the bus.

There wasn't the usual banter among players that Davis—unlike our other coaches—always permitted on these rides. But this seemed an attribute of the game rather than of weather. As we waited, we watched the boosters' concession stand blow down, and shortly after we departed, the wind demolished the grandstand and field lights of our stadium. But we had somewhere to go. As our bus approached the Willamette where we would cross over to the West Side, the trailer end of a sixteen wheeler had been smashed through the railing of the Sellwood Bridge and dangled over the water. We took an alternate route. It was like sitting in the front row of a movie house watching disaster footage. I don't know why we remained so calm, so distanced from what was happening around us. Maybe because there had been no warning. Or because we assumed it would end soon. We passed cars demolished by falling trees, houses with missing roofs, upended telephone booths, and water mains spouting like geysers. Downtown, my stepfather, on leaving his building, was blown into a parking meter that he grasped for safety and that the wind spun him around. In an instant, his hands were lacerated when he nabbed four diamond rings and shards of glass from the shattered window of the adjacent jewelry store.

We were in the midst of a "freak" typhoon, an improbable collision of three weather patterns: the remnants of Typhoon Frieda that had nearly exhausted itself in the China Sea and a system of unusually warm moist air from the southern latitudes that clashed with an extreme cold front from the Gulf of Alaska. The winds raged at a speed in excess of 150 miles per hour, with a velocity through Portland of about 120. The duration of the storm's passage over every point was longer than two hours.

It was after dark and just about game time when our bus entered Beaverton. We had nearly reached our destination, but the congestion and destruction had grown so great that we were unable to continue. Power lines were down across the road. The driver maneuvered the bus into the parking lot of Jesuit High School, and we were motioned inside. Twenty-four Oregonians died as a result of the storm that evening; some for an act as simple as going to the window to see what was happening and having the glass explode and pierce their bodies. The Milwaukie Mustangs took shelter in a rival cafeteria until the early hours of Saturday morning. We feasted on the ice cream that was passed among us. Ice cream bars from the freezers of Jesuit High that, because the power had been off for three hours (it would remain off for nearly a week), had already begun to melt.

14.

Satire: the employment of sarcasm, irony, and ridicule in denouncing, exposing, or deriding vice, folly, abuses, or evils of any kind.

Why confirm the obvious? Because there are ogres in paradise. Because their number expands as the population does. Because the obvious is made obtuse by their language and gesture that tells us that reason is folly and, worse, that folly is reason.

My poems begin as metaphors for experience and are themselves constructed through the use of metaphors and other figures of speech. This sometimes places their subjects far from me. Autobiographical forgery. Picasso put it best: "We all know art is not truth, it is a lie which makes us realize a truth."

15.

I've always respected those who appreciate poetry. When I went through the divorce, my poems were subpoenaed. Ostensibly to prove that I was an unstable person. But the judge, bless her heart, said it wasn't true. As a result I lost only 90 percent of everything I owned.

16.

I was selected to represent my elementary school as a candidate for Rose Festival Prince of the city of Portland. The Rose Festival Parade, held each June, is the culmination of the city's celebration of itself as our nation's "Rose Capital." The first step toward coronation occurred when my classmates and I were escorted by our fourth grade teachers to the gymnasium where we walked slowly in a counterclockwise circle while three ladies, even older than our mothers, ogled. When the two semifinalists were announced, I was one of them. When I got home that afternoon after softball practice, my mother had received the winning phone call. She was ecstatic. A prince! Paul, the other semifinalist, had come over shortly after school because his family had heard nothing. My mother was sorry to have been the one to give him the news.

My early reign was fraught with pressures and difficulties. The next afternoon our candidate for princess, Mary Ann Doss, and I were introduced to the school. The principal was extremely proud of each of us and presented us with boxes designed to look like textbooks that were filled with rolls of assorted Lifesavers and also with identical copies of an illustrated children's story about a horse. Then he took them back so he could present them to us again at the second assembly.

That same week my brother, a second grader, became lodged in the garbage can he had crouched into while playing hide-and-seek at recess. I remember feeling stricken by something I couldn't name while I watched from a third-story window as the two janitors carried him by the handles into the inner courtyard and began to extricate him by hammering at the rivets on the can. I was amazed at how rapidly the news spread over the school grounds. The way a tiny event in a nondescript corner with few witnesses grew to a pilgrimage of custodians with everyone watching. The prince's brother, stuck in a garbage can.

There were the rehearsals on the stage of the Hollywood Theater with the other couples from Rigler and Beaumont and Glen Haven; my mother's borrowing my grandmother's car to transport me there several evenings each week. When I stepped into the spotlight on the big day, I forgot my lines but managed to mumble something about how honored I was. Like the other male contestants, I was wearing a white suit, white shoes, a red bow tie, and a rose boutonniere. My lips were highlighted with lipstick, my ears protruded more than a little, and my hair was combed up and back in the style of the time.

In the parade we rode on a float beneath a huge caricature of Johnny Appleseed made all of roses except for his tin-pan hat. We were interviewed on the radio by Uncle Bob of the "Uncle Bob and the Squirrel Cage" show. This was shortly before his death in that fiery collision of his Triumph while he was on his way to L.A. to take a new job with Disney. A blonde lady in overwhelming perfume had just taught us to wave our arms in a slow arc. "Remember," she said, "you have to keep smiling." We tossed roses to the crowd.

This happened in the spring of 1954. I have the pictures to prove it.

VII.

Excavating the Ruins of Miami Beach

Report from the Past

This is the past,
an intimate diamond,
reappearing.

This is a flame dark
as birth.

This is pleasure
stranger than water
or pain.

This is the voice of
history saying
I keep repeating myself,
please forgive me.

The Story

For years I tried
to write the story called
"Excavating the Ruins of Miami
Beach." I guess I needed
to give some meaning
to that time after the divorce
when my life, all alcohol
and remorse, moved at a pace
far slower than I could adapt
to; one of those times when living
becomes a cruel parody
of our intention.

After ten months,
we were back together—
for who knows what reasons.
We could not live with each other,
then couldn't successfully
live apart. Still there was bitterness.
The accusations. Even deceit. Everything
wreckage and impossibility.

It was the summer we took
our children on that loopy
odyssey across the South
just to avoid the place where trouble
was—at least the part of it
that wasn't us. I think now
we were lucky to live in a country

where you can become someone
else so easily.

* * *

At the south end of Miami Beach,
just off Collins Avenue, beyond
the beautiful seedy tropical Deco hotels
and beside the Adler Burlesque,
years out of its time, the sidewalk
sandwich-board proclaiming *Songstress*
Claire Barry of the Famous "Barry Sisters"
and *Hilarious Comedian Larry Best*
with his Apple Routine—Next Week:
the Vibrant Voice of the Lovely Helen
Marr, was a lunch counter named Big
Daddy's. I walked in,
my four-year-old son on my hand,
and there were the photographs
that made the minute-to-minute
I was living seem less immediate, less
full of consequence, again.
On the walls hundreds of group portraits
of the proprietor and his family alongside
celebrities, all their names stamped out
in tape-gun plastic and affixed
to the frames: Big Daddy, Mrs. Big Daddy,
and the kid—Big Daddy Jr., posed among
Tiny Tim, Johnny Weissmuller, Henny
Youngman, Roland LaStarza, Troy
Donohue, and Dr. Joyce Brothers.

My son at his meal, I roved
the mystical gallery: Myron Cohen, Fabian,
Jack E. Leonard, Frank Sinatra Jr.,
Patty Duke, and José Ferrer. I remember
dreaming, in this land of lunch hour
patrons and the adult incarnation
of Big Daddy Jr. teaching two Vietnamese
boys to wipe down a table, that I
was an archaeologist. I remember laughing.

* * *

I couldn't write
the story, though I lived in it
for a while and was myself
occupied.
     Walking out,
my son eager for his own next episode,·
I understood from the curious half hour
that—hard as I tried—I couldn't solve
any of my problems; and that this,
finally, was how I'd begun
to outgrow them.

Excavating the Ruins of Miami Beach

After months of drilling
and digging, of carving out
the central trench,

they had come down
through layers of soil and cement,
through sand rife with shells—

ample debris of a Cenozoic seabed—
to arrive at the entrance
of a narrow hollow. A phalanx

entering the darkness,
they were astonished, as they lowered
themselves beneath the rotted

ceiling timbers, at the reflections
their lights gave back
of objects fastened to the walls.

Ancient pictographs—
all the artifacts one could covet
in a findspot. The names

had been affixed
in an archaic plastic script,
decipherable in shallow

embossing: Big Daddy and Dr. Erwin
Stillman; Big Daddy and Patty Duke.
This in the midst of something

called a Hot Dog Stand
in the fallen United States. Big
Daddy and Shecky Greene.

Here was the patriarch
in a thousand proofs, his Little
Mama with her buxom personality.

They began to dust and wash
the relics of this fossil beach,
to preserve something

of their own history. Big Daddy
and Norm Crosby. Big Daddy
and Totie Fields and Jerry Vale.

And since this was all they knew—
all this much—
they assumed they knew it all.

The Meeting

Somewhere along the road
you meet up with yourself.
Recognition is immediate.
If it happens at the proper
time and place, you propose
a toast:

May you remain as my shadow
*   when I lie down.*
May I live on as your ghost.

Then you pass, knowing you'll
never see yourself that way
again: the fires that burn
before you are your penance,
the ashes you leave behind are
your name.

IN THE TED KOOSER CONTEMPORARY POETRY SERIES

Darkened Rooms of Summer:
New and Selected Poetry
Jared Carter

The Woods Are On Fire:
New and Selected Poems
Fleda Brown

Rival Gardens:
New and Selected Poetry
Connie Wanek

Regular Haunts:
New and Previous Poems
Gerald Costanzo

To order or obtain more information on these or other University
of Nebraska Press titles, visit nebraskapress.unl.edu.

Lightning Source UK Ltd.
Milton Keynes UK
UKOW04f0559010218
317188UK00001B/119/P